KU-597-354

WHY DID CHRIST DIE?

Study broadcasts by

HERBERT G. WOOD

London

THE EPWORTH PRESS

PUBLISHED BY
THE EPWORTH PRESS
(FRANK H. CUMBERS)
25-35 CITY ROAD, LONDON, E.C.1

*

New York : *Toronto*
Melbourne : *Cape Town*

*

First published 1953

Printed in England by Page & Thomas Ltd.,
Sheraton Street, London, W.1 and at Chesham

PREFACE

The following studies were broadcast on the Midland Home Service early in 1952 in a course entitled 'Reading Your Bible.' They are now printed almost as delivered, but some sentences and paragraphs, which had to be omitted owing to limitation of time, have now been included.

I tender my sincere thanks to authors, or their representatives, for permitting me to use several quotations, among them: 'A.E.' (George Russell) p. 21; Hemingway, *For Whom the Bell Tolls*, p. 34; Gerald Brenan, p. 39 and T. E. Brown's poem, p. 40.

H. G. Wood.

CONTENTS

I

WHY DID CHRIST DIE?

The nature of the question

WHY did Christ die? In this course of study I am inviting you to consider some of the answers given to this question by New Testament writers. I shall try to convince you that there is a wealth of thought concerning the mystery of Christ's death in the pages of the New Testament which cannot be brought within the compass of any one theory of the Atonement. The message of the Cross meant much to the first generation of Christians. In studying the many different values they found in it, we may discover how much it may mean to us today.

In this first study let us consider further the nature of the question to which we seek an answer. Why did Christ die? This is not a simple historical question. We are not enquiring like a detective, or rather as historians into the circumstances under which Jesus of Nazareth was brought to trial and put to death. The phrases in the Apostles' Creed—'suffered under Pontius Pilate, was crucified, dead and buried'—insist on the actuality of the historical event, but we assert the reality of the fact, because the fact or event is fraught with deep meanings and far-reaching consequences. We are concerned with those meanings and consequences. What was the purpose or object of Christ's death? What blessings or benefits has Christ brought to mankind by dying on the Cross?

You will observe that our question is not: Why was *Jesus* put to death? but—Why did *Christ* die? The question could only arise in that form for the first disciples after the message of Easter had created or restored their faith in Jesus as the Christ. The earliest Gospel is not the preaching of the Cross, but the good news of the Resurrection. God has vindicated Jesus; has declared him to be both Christ and Lord, by raising him from the dead. This is the faith on which the Church rests. But men who are convinced that Jesus is the Christ because he is risen from the dead and is alive for evermore, cannot evade the question—Why did Christ die? If God would not suffer his holy one to see corruption, why did he permit him to be put to death by sinful men? There must be some purpose of God in all this. This then, is the earliest Christian conviction concerning the death of Christ. It must have happened in accordance with 'the determinate counsel and foreknowledge of God'. So Peter insists in his address to his Jewish audience at Pentecost. 'Jesus of Nazareth . . . being delivered up by the determinate counsel and foreknowledge of God, ye, by the hand of lawless men, did crucify and slay.' A reference Bible discloses a similar reference to the foreknowledge of God in the opening salutation of the first letter of Peter. This association of the foreknowledge of God with the events of the death of Christ presents many difficulties to our minds. It seems to suggest a pre-conceived drama in which the actors play the parts assigned to them. What then becomes of man's free will and man's responsibility? Let us see if a closer examination of the phrases, with the help of modern versions, will throw any light on the matter. Moffatt's rendering 'betrayed in the predestined course of God's deliberate purpose' leave us very much where we were before. It may even suggest that the betrayal of Jesus by Judas to the Jewish authorities and their subsequent surrender of their prisoner to the Roman proconsul were both parts of God's plan. So indeed Dr. Goodspeed seems to understand it, for he translates—'But you, by the fixed purpose and intention of God, handed him over to wicked men and had him crucified'. Monsignor Knox seems to me to come nearer the real meaning when he writes: 'by God's fixed design and foreknowledge he was *betrayed to you*, and you, through the hands of sinful men, have cruelly murdered him'. But if 'betrayed to you' means 'betrayed by Judas to you', I think this is still not quite right. The word translated 'betrayed', might also be translated 'surrendered' or 'given away',—as a woman is given away by her father or guardian in marriage. What is asserted is not that the action of Judas or the action of the Sanhedrin was in accordance with the will of God, but that God gave away his Son to the mercy of sinful men for them to do what they willed with him.

In this divine surrender, God manifested at the end of the times a purpose and design foreknown from the foundation of the world. So Peter claims in his first epistle (Ch. 3 v. 20).

We are still only at the threshold of our subject. The first believers were sure there must be some purpose of God in Christ's death, and they were the more confident, because they found anticipations of this bewildering event in the Old Testament writings, as we shall see when we study the fundamental thesis—'Christ died for our sins according to the Scriptures'. But though they were sure that there must be some purpose of God in Christ's death, they did not claim to understand it. And as they came to see more and more meanings and values in the Cross, they still felt themselves in the end to be facing a mystery beyond their comprehension. And so it remains. Let Charles Wesley speak for us:

> 'Tis mystery all! Th' Immortal dies!
> Who can explore his strange design!
> In vain the first-born Seraph tries
> To sound the depths of Love Divine!
> 'Tis mercy all; let earth adore,
> Let angel-minds enquire no more.

II

'CHRIST DIED FOR OUR SINS . . . .'

Texts for study: 1 *Cor.* 15^3 *and Acts* 8^{25}

'I HAVE handed on to you among the fundamentals of our faith, the tradition which I too received, how that Christ died for our sins according to the Scriptures.' In writing these words to his friends in Corinth, St. Paul is appealing to the gospel as it was understood and proclaimed by the primitive Church. This is not some peculiar teaching of the apostle. Paul did not invent the Cross, as some moderns seem to think, nor was he the first to discover the paradox of a crucified Messiah.

He may have had—indeed I think he did have—some insight into the meaning of Christ's death which those who were apostles before him did not anticipate and did not at once appreciate. But long before Saul of Tarsus was converted, the first disciples had reached the conviction that Christ died for our sins according to the Scriptures. On this fundamental, Peter and Paul were in full agreement.

On what passages in the Old Testament did the apostles base this conviction? First and foremost, on the Servant-songs of Isaiah, and particularly on the picture of the suffering servant in chapter 53. The full meaning of that amazing chapter dawned on them as they thought over the Passion of their Lord, and the essential purpose of his death became clear to them as they thought over the chapter. Prophecy and history illuminated each other.

The coincidence which first impressed them seems to have been the silence of Jesus in the judgment-hall. When Philip joined the Chamberlain of the Queen of Ethiopia in his chariot, the place of scripture which the traveller was reading was this: 'He was led as a sheep to the slaughter; and as a lamb before his shearer is dumb, so he openeth not his mouth.' 'Beginning from this passage, Philip preached unto him, Jesus.' He may have told the story of the trials and mocking of Jesus very much as Mark tells it. Before the high-priest, Mark says, Jesus kept silence and answered not a word. And so before Pilate, 'Jesus still would not answer, so that Pilate was full of astonishment'. Of course it is possible that Mark's narrative is coloured by this prophecy, but the refusal of Jesus to offer any verbal defence against his accusers is probably historical. There is a reference to Christ's silence in the first letter of Peter which reads like reminiscence of what actually happened, though the chapter from Isaiah is in the writer's mind. 'Christ,' he says, 'suffered on your behalf, leaving you an example that you should follow in the steps of him, who did no sin, in whose mouth was found no guile, who, when he was being reviled, did not answer back, who, while suffering, indulged in no threats but surrendered himself to him who judges justly.' The patience of Jesus, his refusal to defend himself, marks him out as the suffering servant of the Lord. But if the prophecy has been fulfilled in this particular, then the whole chapter becomes relevant and illuminating. Clearly, 'Christ has borne our sins, by his stripes we are healed, we have been redeemed with the precious blood of Christ, as of a lamb without blemish and without spot'. All these expressions in I Peter are derived from Isaiah 53.

The Servant-songs profoundly influenced the thought of the primitive Church. This is apparent from the earliest recorded prayer in Acts 4. It contains the petition that 'signs and wonders may be done through the name of *thy holy Servant* Jesus'. The title 'servant' is also found in the Eucharistic Prayers in *The Teaching of the Twelve Apostles*. There the Christians, when receiving the cup, are directed to give thanks 'for the holy vine . . . which thou hast made known to us through Jesus thy servant'. The same title is used in giving thanks for the breaking of the bread. The usage is certainly primitive.

This identification of Jesus with the suffering servant of Isaiah is not due to the influence of St. Paul, but it may well have been suggested by our Lord Himself. The saying, 'the Son of Man has come not to be served but to serve and to give His life a ransom for many' is manifestly in line with Isaiah 53. The idea of service and ransom are akin to Isaiah's, and the expression 'for many' recalls the passages: 'By his knowledge shall my righteous servant justify *many*,' and 'yet he bare the sin of *many* and made intercession for the transgressors.' There is good ground for believing that our Lord accepted the role of the suffering servant as part of His Messianic vocation.

In the light of Isaiah 53, we can say that 'Christ died for our sins according to Scriptures.' How is this assertion to be interpreted? It is not just that Christ died on account of our sins; that our sins were the cause or occasion of his death. He died for the sake of our sins, to deal with our sins, to free us from our sins. It may suffice at this stage to say, 'He died that we might be forgiven; He died to make us good'.

The relation of Christ's death to the forgiveness of sins will engage our attention later. In I Peter the emphasis is on the thought he died to make us good. He says to his readers: 'You must realise all the time that you have been ransomed from the futile way of living passed on to you by your fathers. Christ bore our sins so that we might be dead to sin and be alive to all that is good.' Christ's death came as a challenge to the ways of the world, as an actual call to repentance. In our next study we must examine the nature of the challenge more closely.

III

THE CHALLENGE OF THE CROSS

Text for study: John 12[33], *Galatians* 3[1]

'I, IF I be lifted up, will draw all men unto Me.' The word translated 'draw' is a forceful one. It is used in Greek of hauling a boat ashore or of dragging unwilling offenders into court. It is used of the compelling attractive power of a magnet. Christ on the Cross will compel attention, will present a challenge that cannot pass unheeded.

St. Paul discovered the drawing-power of the Cross in his own experience. No doubt when he says Christ apprehended or arrested him, he is thinking of what happened on the road to Damascus. But why was he on the road to Damascus at all? Because he could not get away from that strange Man on the Cross. If Christ had not been crucified, Saul of Tarsus would never have persecuted the Church. When this stone of stumbling became for Paul the one foundation, he determined to preach only Christ crucified. God's power worked through this gospel. He was astonished when men failed to respond. 'O foolish Galatians, who hath bewitched you—you before whose very eyes

Jesus Christ was placarded, crucified!' Rendel Harris once spoke of Paul, as the bill-poster. The preaching of the apostle was like a startling advertisement. But the arresting power was in the theme and this is God-designed. The Cross arrests and attracts when organised Christianity repels.

We sometimes pray, 'Oh, speak and make me listen, Thou guardian of my soul'. But Christ has spoken and He died to make us listen. What was the message to which He would compel our attention? It has been well said that 'Jesus had no occasion to attach to His death any special object beyond that served by His whole activity. He died in order to be able to do in eternal perfection that which He was always doing: namely, to call men to repent, to forgive, to set men free by making visible the majesty of God's mercy.' Look again at the saying, 'The Son of Man has come not to be served, but to serve and to give His life a ransom for many'. His giving of His life is the culmination of His earthly ministry. It completes and perfects His service to mankind. The call to repentance takes its final form in His suffering and death.

Reflect for a minute or two on this aspect of the Cross. Christ died in a special sense for Israel, to awake them to the danger in which they stood through the growing tension between Rome and Jewry. 'Except ye repent, ye shall all likewise perish.' 'Daughters of Jerusalem, weep not for Me; weep for yourselves.' Christ died in the attempt to avert disaster from Israel. But the Cross stood as a challenge to the futile way of living traditional in the Gentile world. 'Their great ones exercise lordship : it shall not be so among you.' Christ died to change the world's standards of greatness. His death strikes at the root of our pride and love of power.

In his Apologia, Cardinal Newman drew a sombre picture of the anarchical self-frustrated condition of human society. He asked what form a divine interposition might be expected to take, 'supposing it were the blessed and loving will of the Creator to intervene', so as 'to withstand the fierce energy of passion and the all-corroding, all-dissolving scepticism of the intellect in religious enquiries'. The fundamental form of such divine intervention is surely the Cross itself—the theme of Newman's hymn, 'Praise to the Holiest in the height'. Like the mariner's compass ever pointing to the magnetic north, the function of the Church is to point men to the Christ uplifted on the Cross who will draw all men to Himself.

Here is God's challenge alike to the fierce energy of passion and to the scepticism of the intellect. The challenge is inescapable, but it is not at once acceptable. Men resent and reject it. We must then consider the offence of the Cross.

IV

THE OFFENCE OF THE CROSS

Text for study: *I Corinthians* 1[18]

I SHALL preface what I have to say on our main theme, with a few suggestions for private study. A serious Bible-student should use a good reference Bible and should have a concordance readily available. The same word may not have exactly the same meaning in every context and the same English word may not always represent the same Greek or Hebrew. Nevertheless Scripture-parallels and Scripture-associations are an indispensable aid to the understanding of particular passages. The best commentary on the Scriptures is still to be found in the Scriptures themselves. Then the many modern versions often bring out the true significance of verses and phrases, which have ceased to move us either because they are staled by familiarity or because they are obscured by inadequate or archaic renderings. But a translation, new or old, is often a commentary or paraphrase rather than an exact translation.

We need to check the versions by consulting the best commentators at our disposal. In some ways, the profoundest interpretations are contained in the hymn book. It was said of T. R. Glover that when he found himself out of his depth in discussing the doctrine of the Atonement, he would say, 'Let's sing a hymn.' This might be a shirking of mental effort, but it might also be the road to true understanding. Keep the hymn-book by you. Beyond this we must be on the look-out for illustrations from life and literature.

Now let us turn to our theme, the offence of the Cross. 'The word or message of the Cross is foolishness to them that are perishing, but to us who are being saved it is God's power.' St. Paul is not here dividing mankind into two classes, the lost and the saved—classes whose limits are fixed and whose members are known. The participles are present participles—those who are in danger of being lost, not 'those who are doomed to perish' as one modern version has it, 'us who are being saved', not 'us who are to be saved' as another modern version puts it. The ideas of election and predestination which have their place in 'Romans' are not relevant here. St. Paul is not asserting that those who are on the way to destruction must inevitably be lost, or that those who are on the way to salvation will assuredly be saved. The first may still repent, the second may still fall away. What the apostle is saying comes to this, 'So long as the message of the Cross is folly in our eyes, we are in danger of eternal loss. If we find in the Cross the wisdom and power of God, we are in the way of salvation.'

Why does the message of the Cross offend? St. Paul goes on to explain. 'The Jews require a sign, and the Greeks seek after wisdom, but we preach Christ crucified, unto the Jews a stumbling-block and unto the Greeks, foolishness.' The offence to the Jews of the first century is readily understood. A crucified

Messiah is a contradiction in terms, the flat denial of the hopes the Jews associated with the coming of Messiah. They expected a Messiah ushered in by signs from heaven and endowed with miraculous powers to overthrow their oppressors. That they were offended in Jesus is not surprising. A teacher condemned as unorthodox by the Sanhedrin and subjected to a punishment to which a divine curse is attached in the Law, cannot be the Christ. St. Paul knew what he was talking about when he said the Cross was a stumbling-block to the Jews. He had stumbled over it himself.

If to Jews the association of the Cross with the Christ seemed incredible, to the Greeks the association of suffering with the divine seemed unthinkable. No dogma was more firmly fixed in the Greek philosophic mind than this, God cannot suffer. In one of Lucian's witty *Dialogues of the Dead*, King Philip of Macedon upbraids his son, Alexander the Great, for repudiating his human father and claiming to be the son of Zeus. When Alexander says, 'Have you nothing to say of my adventurous spirit when I led an attack and was covered with wounds?' Philip replies, 'That would be all very well for a king's son, but this was the last thing *you* were called upon to do. You were passing for a God, and your being wounded and carried off the field in a litter, bleeding and groaning, could only excite the ridicule of the spectators. The son of Zeus in a swoon, requiring medical assistance! Who could help laughing at the sight!'

Obviously the word of the Cross will be folly to Lucian. At a later date, a better representative of the Greek mind, the Neoplatonist, Porphyry takes a similar line. He quotes an oracle given to a man who asked to what God he should sacrifice to obtain his wife's conversion from Christianity. Apollo gave the poor man little encouragement. It is almost impossible to reclaim a woman from such an infatuation. 'Let her run after her empty foolish opinions as long as she likes: let her honour with misguided lamentations her dead God whom the wise and well-advised judges condemned and whom a shameful death upon the Cross despatched.' Porphyry endorses the oracle and declares that the Jews maintain God's honour better than the Christians.

Is this only past history or are the Greeks still with us? Is there something of the Greek in each one of us which rejects the message of the Cross as foolishness? Evidence of such an attitude among our literary and intellectual guides is not far to seek. We need only look again at Shaw's preface to Androcles and the Lion, and especially at the paragraph on 'The Right to refuse Atonement'. A simpler illustration may suffice —some lines from a poem by the Irish poet 'A.E.'

> The worship of the dead is not
> A worship that our hearts allow,
> Though every famous shade were wrought
> With woven thorns above the brow.

But here we have to reckon with sentimental perverted devotions and with crude vulgar presentations of the message of the Cross which offend not only our reason but our taste and our moral sensibility. Shaw's critique of what he called Salvationism had some justification. Yet there was in Shaw and there is in the modern mind a resentment of the whole idea of Christ as mediator, an unwillingness to admit that Christ in dying has done something for us which we could not do for ourselves. For this reason the intelligentsia of today dismiss St. Paul's preaching of Christ crucified, without trying seriously to understand it. What did Paul mean by declaring that the Cross is the power of God unto Salvation? In our next three studies we must address ourselves to this question.

V

CHRIST'S DEATH, GOD'S WAY OF SAVING A SICK SOCIETY

Text for study: *Romans* 3^{21-26}

'I AM ready to preach the Gospel to you that are in Rome also. For I am not ashamed of the gospel: it is the power of God unto salvation to every one that believeth.' To preach the message of the Cross in Rome, the heart of the Empire, required courage. In the eyes of a Roman, like the historian Tacitus, Christianity was a pestilential superstition, and Christ, a Jewish fanatic who had been put to death during the reign of Tiberius by the procurator, Pontius Pilate, and who had suffered the most ignominious and cruel form of death penalty, the form reserved for slaves and rebels. Paul might well be ashamed to plead for faith in a crucified Christ as the Saviour of the Roman world! But he wasn't. He was full of confidence in his gospel. It is the power of God unto salvation.

From what did he suppose the Roman world needed to be saved? He starts with a description of a world under the wrath of God. Men need to be saved from the wrath of God. What did Paul mean by this phrase?

The prophets had often seen the wrath of God in

natural calamity, in military defeat and political disaster. When John the Baptist warns folk to flee from the wrath to come, he is probably like Amos anticipating the violent overthrow of the existing social and political order. Christian evangelists spoke much of a last judgement and of punishments in a life after death. St. Paul will speak of the wrath to come in similar terms, but here in Romans, chapter I, the emphasis is different. Professor Klausner described Graeco-Roman society in the first century A.D. as 'a world decaying for lack of God and social morality'. So St. Paul saw it. Men had forgotten God and devoted themselves to idols. They had taken God's good gifts for granted and had ceased to be thankful. From this practical atheism followed the breakdown of social morality. Moral corruption saps the mind and men were losing even the ability to distinguish right from wrong. In this actual process of moral and intellectual deterioration God's wrath is manifested. Vice becomes its own punishment. If men are to be saved from the wrath, this process of decay must be arrested and reversed.

'The death of Socrates,' Lord Lindsay of Birker once observed, 'stopped the moral rot in Greece.' At least it stemmed the process of decay, since it convinced many young men that truth and justice were no playthings, but realities worth dying for. So St. Paul saw in the death of Christ, God's way of stopping the moral rot of the Roman world. Since he thought the end of the age was close at hand, he may not have expected to salvage civilisation. The most he could hope for was that believers would be saved from being engulfed in the ruin of a social order. God would deliver them from the kingdom of darkness and transfer them to the kingdom of his beloved Son. Yet as these little

Christian cells, these little outposts or colonies of heaven, multiplied and grew, the body politic might be renewed and transformed. If the presence of ten righteous men might have saved Sodom and Gomorrah, what might not the spread of the Gospel do for the Roman World?

Here then is the problem:—a world decaying for lack of God and social morality—how is it to be saved?

The moralist, Stoic or Pharisee, is ready with an answer—more ethical precepts, more laws, a new code. But the moralist imagines that he stands outside and above this festering corrupt society, and he thinks to save society by preaching to it from outside. The apostle challenges this. He thinks the moralist is involved in the process and needs to be saved like everybody else. The remedy for sin is something more costing than a new code of law. And so we come to our key passage in chapter 3. Let us read it now in Dr. Moffatt's version.

'But now we have a righteousness of God disclosed apart from law altogether; it is attested by the law and the prophets, but it is a righteousness of God which comes by believing in Jesus Christ. And it is meant for all who have faith. No distinctions are drawn. All have sinned, all come short of the glory of God, but they are justified for nothing by His grace through the ransom provided in Christ Jesus, whom God put forward as the means of propitiation by His blood, to be received by faith. This was to demonstrate the justice of God in view of the fact that sins previously committed during the time of God's forbearance had been passed over: it was to demonstrate His justice at the present epoch, showing that God is just Himself and that He justifies man on the score of faith in Jesus.'

You will realise that this is a most difficult passage,

and we shall not exhaust it in three brief studies. This at least is clear. The remedy for sin is to be found in a new revelation of God's righteousness, a revelation embodied in a person, not just enacted in a code. To be delivered from the dominion of darkness, men must come to know God in a new way. A divine intervention is needed, both to convince men of God's righteousness and to set them on the way of moral recovery. To convince men of God's righteousness—on this point in verse 25, Dr. Moffatt seems to me nearer to Paul's thought than the Authorised Version. The disclosure of God's righteousness through Christ's death is not needed 'for the remission of sins that are past, through the forbearance of God,' as the Authorised Version says, but, as Dr. Moffatt says, 'in view of the fact that sins previously committed during the time of God's forbearance had been passed over'. Men interpreted God's patient forbearance as indifference or as an easy-going indulgence which would give them impunity. And for the more sensitive the question was irrepressible: Does God really care? Here is a world collapsing in sin—why does not God do something about it? Habakkuk's agonised question requires an answer. 'Thou that art of purer eyes than to behold evil and that canst not look on perverseness, wherefore lookest thou upon them that deal treacherously, and holdest thy peace when the wicked swalloweth up the man that is more righteous than he?' So many of us asked during the war, why does not God do something to stop it? Why does he not do something to deliver us from the peril of World War III? The answer is, God has done something, He has done the one thing needed. Christ died to convince us that God does care and to show us how God cares. On this conviction our hopes of personal salvation and social renewal depend.

The death of Christ did not avert the tragedy of the Jewish wars. The preaching of the Cross did not prevent the decline and fall of the Roman Empire. Gibbon indeed thought that Christianity hastened the process. He drew an idealised picture of the happiness and prosperity of the Roman World under the Antonines, and in tracing the subsequent decline he thought he was describing the triumph of barbarism and religion. But as Arnold Toynbee has shown, Gibbon mistook the flush on the cheek of a consumptive for the bloom of health. Already in the second century the process of inner decay was far advanced. The gospel did not save the old society, but it formed the Church, which stood when the old order fell and which in time created the first Europe.

Today we live in a world decaying for lack of God and morality, social and international. Science alone will not save us. We need to know God, and Christ died to bring to us the knowledge we need. He died to save us from the kind of catastrophe we all fear. Whether the breakdown of our civilisation will be averted we cannot be sure, but there is no other name whereby we may be saved.

VI

THE GOSPEL OF THE CROSS AND THE RELIGION OF LAW

Text for study: Romans 10[4]

'CHRIST is the end of the law for righteousness to every one that believeth.' This carries on the thought of last week's key passage: 'But now we have a righteousness of God disclosed, apart from law altogether.' For St. Paul the death of Christ means that the religion of law is dead and done with. To adopt Monsignor Knox's version, 'Christ has superseded the law'.

This is St. Paul's most original contribution to the interpretation of the Cross. It was not easily understood by his contemporaries. It is not easily understood today. To proclaim a righteousness which is to be attained apart from law altogether, seems to open the door to those forms of religious enthusiasm which sit loose to morality. The apostle did not intend this, but he was so misinterpreted in his lifetime. Many have thought that he must have meant that Christ has fulfilled the law for us, not that Christ superseded it. Yet St. Paul nowhere suggests that Christ strictly observed the law. But he does say that Christ's death satisfied and ended a claim which the law has on all its subjects. In a rather confused comparison in Romans 7 he compares the relation between the law and Christian believers to the relation of husband and wife, which ends with the death of either of the partners. He should have said that the husband, the law, has died and released the wife to be wedded to Christ. Instead he says 'the crucified body of Christ made you dead to the law'. The dead wife apparently is free to marry again! Though the comparison is confused, the meaning is clear. The Law has no claim on the Christian believer.

The same thought is expressed in Galatians, chapter 3, where St. Paul recalls the curse pronounced on those who fail to keep the Law, and then adds 'Christ redeemed us from the curse of the Law, having become a curse for us—for it is written, Cursed be everyone who hangs on a tree'. This may seem a strange argument, but it had a vital significance for St. Paul. The thought that anyone who died on a cross was under the curse of the Law had been a great obstacle to the recognition of Jesus as the Christ. Now St. Paul sees a divine purpose in it. Christ, by dying in this manner, takes upon him the curse pronounced in the Law and exhausts it. The Law's claim on defaulting humanity has been paid in full.

Still we might say, Christ's death would not thereby end the Law. Did not St. Paul mean that Christ's death has wiped out our past debt and enables us to start again with a clean balance-sheet under the old rules? Since he regards the Law as holy and just and good, can he have supposed that it was superseded? But this is precisely what he did suppose. The forgiven sinner does not start again under the old rules. He lives on a new basis.

Another way of minimising the apostle's daring assertion is to suggest that he was thinking of Judaism as a legal religious system and insisting that as a system it is ended. The ceremonial ritual elements were brought to an end by Christ's death. The moral law must have been reaffirmed. There is some truth in this, but it misses St. Paul's point. The Law as a moral discipline was to his mind only a temporary expedient. He was acutely aware of the weakness of every form of legal religion, of every attempt to reform and save men by telling them, Not to do this and Not to do that. He might have sympathised with those who say, You cannot make men good by Act of Parliament! He was impressed by the moral powerlessness of the Law. 'If a Law had been given which could make alive, then righteousness would indeed be by the Law and Christ need not have died.' But the Law, weakened by the flesh, cannot make alive, cannot make men righteous.

St. Paul must have had misgivings about the religion of Law before he faced the challenge of the Cross. In his experience the Law, particularly in its negative precepts, 'Thou shalt not', evoked resistance and set up inner conflict. When the Law said, 'Thou shalt not covet', he forthwith began to covet. The Law seems to prompt men to sin rather than to save them from it. Contra-suggestible folk will understand this at once!

It is important to note that by the flesh, St. Paul did not mean merely our unruly physical appetites, but much rather the self-centred self-assertive attitude of mind. He found that his Pharisaic ideal of righteousness through strict observance of the Law was deepening his self-centredness. A righteousness of one's own means that under the Law we live as servants in our great Taskmaster's eye, and if we can present our true account, we claim our reward as of right. But a self-made saint may be as disagreeable as many a self-made man, and in the end the relation to God, the relation of Lord and servant, will be profoundly unsatisfying. Moreover, it was precisely his zeal for the Law that led Saul of Tarsus to persecute the Church. It was precisely their zeal for the Law that led his fellow-countrymen to reject the Christ when He came. They had a zeal for God, but it was not enlightened. In short, the Law, though holy and just and good, had not brought men the true knowledge of God and His will. In the light of the Cross, the religion of Law is seen to have failed as a way of salvation.

Christ died then so that we should no longer live as meticulous anxious servants of a taskmaster-God, but as the care-free children of our Father in heaven. In justice to the followers of the religion of Law, we must remember that service and sonship were not so sharply contrasted and separated by the writer of Psalm 119 for example as they were by St. Paul. The Apostle too was under law to Christ and gloried in being Christ's slave. But it makes a profound difference whether we are children first and serve God as children rather than as slaves. Do we hope eventually to be treated as sons because of our faithful service, or do we serve faithfully and joyously because God treats us as sons and because God has sent the spirit of His Son into our hearts, crying Abba! Father? If St. Paul was right, the first alternative is illusory, and the second describes our standing and experience as believers in Christ.

Christ supersedes the Law. We do not need precepts and codes when we have Christ's example and the leading of His Spirit. The forbidding negations of the Law are replaced by Christ's encouraging affirmations. As Dora Greenwell wrote,

Thou bringest all again: with Thee
  Is light, is space, is breadth and room
For each thing fair, belov'd and free
  To have its hour of life and bloom.

To be saved, we need to be delivered from our self-centredness. No code of Law can do this. It requires what Thomas Chalmers called the expulsive power of a great affection. If we realised what we owe to Christ, we should live out our lives from a new centre. Christ would become our true self. But what do we owe to Christ? We may get further light on this in considering man's need of expiation and Christ's death in relation to it.

VII

CHRIST'S DEATH AND MAN'S NEED OF EXPIATION

Text for study: *Romans* 3^{25}

'CHRIST JESUS whom God put forward as a means of propitiation by His blood, to be received by faith.' So Moffatt renders Romans, Chapter 3, v. 25, following the Authorised Version in retaining the term 'propitiation'. The word here translated 'propitiation' is infrequent in the New Testament, but like the verse in Romans the passages are important. There are two passages in the First Epistle of John, where a word from the same root appears. Both times the Authorised version and Moffatt agree in the rendering 'propitiation'. 'Christ is Himself the propitiation for our sins', and 'God loved us and sent his Son to be the propitiation for our sins'. But in all three places, the American revised version substitutes the word 'expiation'. The change reflects closer study of the use of the word in the Greek version of the Old Testament.

You will ask, is the change from 'propitiation' to 'expiation' so important? What difference does it make? The difference is important. The word 'propitiation' suggests doing something to placate the anger of someone who has been offended. From this suggestion arise the ideas that Christ's sacrifice of Himself was needed to appease God's wrath or satisfy God's justice or maintain God's honour. The word is never so used in the Old Testament, and it is doubtful whether this idea of propitiation has any place in the New Testament. The word 'expiation' suggests something done to cleanse us from the stain and pollution of sin, to ease the burden of a guilty conscience.

It may, however, be as difficult for us today to accept the idea of expiation as to retain the idea of propitiation. Psychologists and humanists are inclined to dismiss the sense of sin and the feeling of guilt as morbid and irrational. Undoubtedly much unhappiness and mental illness are occasioned by feelings of guilt which spring from an over-scrupulous or ill-informed conscience. The psychiatrist can minister to a mind diseased. But whether we shall achieve happiness by refusing to regard ourselves as miserable sinners, is more dubious. For there are feelings of guilt which arise inevitably when we face reality, and to dismiss them as morbid betrays insensitiveness—a lack of intelligence as well as hardness of heart. If by reflection or in some moment of vision we become aware of the holiness of God, we shall be overwhelmed, as the prophet Isaiah was in the Temple, by a sense of our unworthiness. We shall say as he said, 'I am a man of unclean lips and I dwell among a people of unclean lips.' Guilt and the need of expiation arise not because God is angry, but because He is Holy.

The poet Wordsworth reported a similar reaction to a less definite awareness of the supernatural when he gave thanks 'for those obstinate questionings of sense and outward things, Fallings from us, vanishings;

Blank misgivings of a creature, Moving about in worlds not realised, High instincts before which our mortal Nature Did tremble like a guilty thing surprised'. Psycho-analysis doesn't begin to explain the experience of the prophet or the poet. If their sense of guilt seems to us morbid, it is because the shades of the prison-house have closed in on us, and the vision which might have been the master-light of all our seeing has faded into the light of common day.

Again, the sense of guilt arises inevitably and rationally if, as someone said recently, 'we are old enough to remember that there is an absolute distinction between right and wrong and if we do not underestimate the weight of sin'. Ernest Hemingway in his novel *For Whom the Bell Tolls* provides an illustration in the Republican partisan, Anselmo, as he stands sentinel. 'I hope I am not for the killing,' Anselmo was thinking. 'I think that after the war there will have to be some great penance done for the killing. If we no longer have religion after the war, then I think there must be some form of civic penance organised that all may be cleansed from the killing or else we will never have a true and human basis for living. The killing is necessary, I know, but still the doing of it is very bad for a man—anyone doing it will be brutalised in time—and I think that after all this is over . . . there must be a penance of some kind for the cleansing of us all.' There would be more hope for us if we all thought as Anselmo did, if we were more ashamed of what we have done in two world wars and less afraid of what may happen in a third world war. We have not yet found a true and human basis for living.

The kind of civic penance advocated by Anselmo would be worth organising, but it might be formal and could never be adequate. Important as it is, that we should make what reparation is in our power when we have done wrong, yet sooner or later we realise that we cannot truly expiate our sins. We begin to realise why Toplady wrote:

> Could my zeal no respite know,
> Could my tears for ever flow,
> All for sin could not atone,
> Thou must save and Thou alone.

C. H. Dodd in his comment on the references to expiation in the first epistle of John puts the matter thus: 'The Gospel speaks to our condition when it assures us not only that God loves the world and is ready to forgive our sins, but that His love has been expressed concretely and objectively in history to provide a means of sterilising human wickedness and effecting a forgiveness which is not merely an amnesty or indulgence, but a radical removal of the taint. We may not be able to give a fully reasoned theology of the matter, but we are entitled to believe in the face of the degradation of our common humanity, that God has done in Christ all that needs to be done to cleanse us, and done it with the complete adequacy possible only to infinite power and love.'

We have to be humble enough to accept forgiveness and to recognise that Christ has done something for us which we cannot do for ourselves. For as Grace Stuart points out in her book *Conscience and Reason*, our altruistic acts, if done to ease a sense of guilt and unworthiness, are still self-related, tainted with anxiety about ourselves. Our acts of reparation are as vain as the sacrifices prescribed in the old Law. They do not effectively cleanse the conscience, or lift the burden of guilt. They become the dead works from which, as the writer to the Hebrews says, the blood of Christ cleanses the conscience, setting us free to serve the living God—to serve without a self-regarding reference. Because Christ is the expiation for our sins and for the sins of the whole world, we can, not only come boldly to the throne of grace to find succour in time of need, but we can retain our hope for mankind and devote ourselves selflessly to the welfare of our fellows.

VIII

CHRIST SHARES THE BURDEN OF OUR MORTALITY

Text for study: *Hebrews* $2^{8\text{-}18}$, *especially verse* 9

WHEN we turn to the letter to the Hebrews, we find a somewhat different approach to our main theme. The writer is concerned to present Jesus to us as our merciful and faithful high-priest, who represents us to God and God to us. But if Jesus is to be our high-priest, He must be in all things like His brethren. He must participate in our nature of flesh and blood. He must share with us and bear for us the burden of our mortality. So the writer declares that it was worthy of God that He should equip fully the captain of our salvation through sufferings. It was fitting that through the grace of God Jesus should taste death for every man.

What is worthy of God must be true of Him, but it is not easy for us to judge what is worthy of God. Theology, orthodox and unorthodox, is strewn with the errors of men who too confidently assumed that they knew what was worthy of God and so could deduce what was true of Him. Hooker rightly reminded the

Puritans that 'in matters which concern the actions of God, the most dutiful way on our part is to search what God hath done and in meekness to admire that, rather than to dispute what He in congruity of reason ought to do'. Before Good Friday, we may be sure that few, if any, would have regarded the Crucifixion as worthy of God. Before the event, we should all have said with Peter, This be far from Thee, Lord! It is only after the event that we begin in meekness to admire what God hath done.

We can see now that it was worthy of God to equip Jesus as our Leader and Saviour through sufferings. Like us, Jesus had to walk by faith. Note the significance of the quotation in verse 13 of Hebrews, chapter 2. 'I will put my trust in Him.' Like his brethren, Jesus puts his trust in God. As a 17th-century Puritan divine said, 'He was the greatest believer that ever lived'. He learned obedience by the things that He suffered. He could not represent us and He could not succour us if He had not shared our experience of temptation and trouble. We have not a high-priest who cannot be touched with the feeling of our infirmities, but one who has been tempted at all points in virtue of His likeness to us, yet without sin. To crown all, through the grace of God He tasted death for every man.

We are led to reflect again on the manner of Christ's death. Why should the death on the Cross be peculiarly fitting, peculiarly worthy of God. Christ died a shameful, violent death at the hands of His enemies. Why should He die in that way rather than in any other? The passage in Hebrews suggests the answer. Only so could He taste death *for every man.* For we must insist, that He died not only for those who believe in Him but for all men, for each and all of us. There is no one who is condemned to suffer the death penalty—whether justly like the two bandits who were crucified along with Him, or unjustly as so many have perished in our time at the hands of political opponents—there is no one, I say, who when compelled to face this manner of death, may not draw comfort and courage from the thought that his Saviour has been through this on his behalf before him.

Again, if the original form of Isaac Watt's hymn be, as is sometimes supposed, 'When I survey the wondrous Cross, Where the *young* Prince of glory died', this recalls another feature of Christ's death which is worth pondering. We are told that Jesus was about 30 years old when He began His ministry and the ministry lasted, at the most, three years. He died in the full vigour of His manhood. If in dying Christ put Himself alongside the criminal, the slave and the victim of political conflict, He also came close to all who are cut off in the flower of their youth. But whether we be young or old, whether we die a natural death or are put to death by violence, it is true for all of us that

> Christ takes us through no darker rooms
> Than He went through before.

No wonder the writer to the Hebrews thought that since Christ shares the burden of our mortality, He frees us from bondage to the fear of death.

Another aspect of our main theme is suggested by a passage in Mr. Gerald Brenan's book *The Face of Spain*. Mr. Brenan travelled to Spain by air, and he writes: 'Flying induces a mood of religious scepticism. One realises the fallacy of supposing that God can be "up above" and can "Look down" on us. For the view of the observer up above is necessarily one of indifference. One sees a man bicycling, one sees a little farm with its stream and bridge, and they have nothing human about them. One does not wish to help the man on his road or to drop a blessing on the little house. To feel well or ill disposed towards them one must see them horizontally, on the level. Man can only be man to those who walk on the earth beside him.' Mr. Brenan describes a *mood* of religious scepticism rather than a rational doubt, for the mood rests on a fallacy—the fallacy of supposing that if God be above and beyond us, He must, as Epicurus taught, be indifferent to us. But this mood of religious scepticism suggests a reason for the Incarnation. Only through a merciful and faithful high-priest, to whom our full humanity belongs could God meet us and deal with us on the level.

Professor Gwatkin used to say 'A God who cannot be touched with the feeling of our infirmities is inferior to a dog which can!' By the grace of God Jesus tasted death for every man that we might never imagine God to be indifferent to our pains and sorrows. In thus assuming the burden of our mortality, Jesus represents God to us. God is not just up above, He is with us. The writer to the Hebrews, I think, might have approved the closing verses of T. E. Brown's poem, 'Pain'. After speaking of our threefold oneness with the One, the poet concludes:

> But tenfold one is he, who feels all pains,
> Not partial, knowing them
> As ripples parted from the gold-beaked stem,
> Wherewith God's galley onward ever strains.
>
> To him the sorrows are the tension thrills
> Of that serene endeavour,
> Which yields to God for ever and for ever
> The joy that is more ancient than the hills.

IX

CHRIST'S DEATH AND THE NEW COVENANT

Text for study: *Mark* 14[24]

IN Mark's account of the Lord's last supper with His disciples we read that 'He took a cup and when He had given thanks He gave it to them and they all drank of it. And He said to them, This is My blood of the covenant, which is poured out for many'. The form of the saying is varied slightly in the first letter to Corinthians (chapter 11, v. 25). It runs 'This cup is the new covenant in My blood'.

Whenever the first Christians met to break bread together and to re-enact the scene in the upper room, they linked the Lord's death with the new covenant. The link had been forged by our Lord Himself in what He said when He distributed the bread and passed round the cup. He likened His approaching death to the sacrifice of the Passover lamb. That sacrifice had been the means of a great deliverance. It made possible the exodus from bondage in Egypt, and the establishment of the old covenant whereby Jehovah became the God of Israel and Israel became his people. Christ's death would accomplish a greater deliverance, a deliverance from sin and the fear of death for all who put their trust in Him. His blood soon to be shed for many—that is, for all mankind—would bring into being that new covenant, the terms of which had been unfolded in memorable words by the prophet Jeremiah.

'This is the covenant which I will make with the house of Israel after those days, says the Lord : I will put my laws into their minds and write them on their hearts and I will be their God and they shall be my people. And they shall not teach every one his fellow or every one his brother, saying, Know the Lord : for all shall know Me from the least of them to the greatest. For I will be merciful to their iniquities and I will remember their sins no more.'

That Christ died to establish the new covenant is a primitive Christian conviction. The most elaborate comment on the theme is to be found in the letter to the Hebrews. In chapter 9, verses 15 to 18, the writer speaks of the death of Christ as a kind of ratification of the new covenant in His blood. It betokens an irrevocable commitment. To strengthen his case for the necessity of Christ's death, the writer to the Hebrews apparently plays on the double meaning of the word which is used in the Greek version of the Old Testament to translate the Hebrew word for covenant. The Greek word in question normally means last will and testament. Presumably the Greek translators used it to represent covenant or agreement, because in a covenant or agreement between God and men, the parties to the covenant are not equal. The initiative is with God, not with men. God establishes the covenant and invites men to join with Him. It is as much God's act, as a man's last will and testament is the act and deed of the man who makes the will. To this day we speak of the old and new testaments, though we mean the old and new covenants. So the writer to the Hebrews, when he speaks of Jesus as the mediator of a new covenant, continues, 'where a will is involved, the death of the one who made it must be established. For a will takes effect only at death, since it is not in force as long as the one who made it is alive.' This apparent confusion of covenant and will proves too much. It is true that a will only takes effect when the testator dies, but a covenant lapses if the one who makes it dies. But what the writer is concerned to argue is that God is irrevocably committed to the new covenant. Covenants have often been signed in blood. So in Christ's blood shed for many, he sees God's signature to the new covenant. The new covenant is as unalterable as the terms of a will after the death of the testator.

In a later passage in Hebrews, the readers are assured that they have come to Jesus the mediator of a new covenant and to the sprinkled blood that speaks more graciously than the blood of Abel. Possibly a parallel is suggested with the blood of the Passover lamb which, sprinkled on the doorposts of the homes of the Israelites, protected them from the angel of death. But earlier the writer refers to the occasion when, after reading the law, the book of the old covenant, Moses purified the book and the tabernacle and the people by sprinkling them with sacrificial blood. So he says our hearts are to be sprinkled clean from an evil conscience. But the contrast with the blood of Abel is even more illuminating. The blood of Abel spilled on the ground called for vengeance and punishment. The blood of Christ calls for mercy and forgiveness. A simple footnote might be supplied by what happened when Count Bernadotte was assassinated. We were not asked to avenge his murder, but to contribute to the work of the

Red Cross. Christ's sprinkled blood is the supreme assurance of forgiveness. Well might John Wesley translate J. A. Rothe's hymn:

> Now I have found the ground wherein
> Sure my soul's anchor may remain:
> The wounds of Jesus for my sin,
> Before the world's foundation slain;
> Whose mercy shall unshaken stay,
> When heaven and earth are passed away.

If Christ's death is the pledge of free forgiveness it is also an appeal to us to be endlessly forgiving. It is a direct challenge to all those who would shut the gates of mercy on mankind.

If the forgiveness of sins is an essential feature of the new covenant, so too is the promise of a communion with God not dependent on the testimony of others, however much it may be helped by their witness, and enriched by the communion of saints. The new covenant is the answer to the prayer of Thomas à Kempis, 'Speak, Lord, for Thy servant heareth. Let not Moses speak unto me, nor any of the prophets, but rather do Thou speak, O Lord God, Inspirer and Enlightener of all the prophets: for Thou alone without them canst perfectly instruct me, but they without Thee can profit nothing.'

The new covenant likewise includes the realisation of the hope of the poet Wordsworth, that the time would come when 'love would be an unerring light and joy its own security'. And Jesus is the mediator of the covenant in which the prayer of Thomas à Kempis is answered and the hope of Wordsworth realised.

X

CHRIST'S DEATH, CHRIST'S GLORY

Text for study: John 7^{39}

THE evangelists are for the most part sparing in comment. They are content to let the sayings and incidents they record make their own impression. Mark does indeed underline the importance of Christ's saying, 'Nothing from without can defile a man', by adding, 'Thus he declared all foods clean'. But comments of this kind are rare in Mark. The fourth evangelist more frequently offers such interpretations. One of the most remarkable of these comments is to be found in John, chapter 7, verse 39. The evangelist has just recorded the saying, 'If any one thirst, let him come to Me and drink. He who believes in Me, as the Scripture has said, 'Out of his heart shall flow rivers of living water.' Then follows this striking comment. 'Now this He said about the Spirit, which those who believed in Him were to receive; for as yet the Spirit had not been given because Jesus was not yet glorified.' This is the earliest reference in the gospel to Jesus being glorified. What is meant by the expression, and how is the gift of the Spirit bound up with the glorification of Jesus?

Naturally, our minds turn first to scenes like The Transfiguration or the Ascension, or to the picture of the Son of Man seated on His throne of glory and judging mankind. But the fourth evangelist has a different association of ideas. As we read on, references to Jesus being glorified become more frequent and almost invariably they seem to be associated with Christ's death. Christ is glorified not so much on the mount of Transfiguration as on Calvary. We have not to wait for Him to appear in glory to judge mankind; He already reigns from the Tree. The Cross is itself the throne of glory. The crucifixion is Christ's exaltation.

This association of ideas is clear in chapter 12. When Philip and Andrew tell their Master of the Greeks who asked to see Him, He answers, 'The hour has come for the Son of Man to be glorified. Truly, truly, I say to you, unless a grain of wheat falls into the earth and dies, it abides alone; but if it dies, it bears much fruit.' Clearly the hour has come for the Son of Man to die, and so to be glorified. The reference to the death of Christ may not at once be apparent in the previous chapter, where Jesus says of the illness of Lazarus, 'This illness is not unto death; it is for the glory of God so that the Son of God may be glorified by means of it.' The reader naturally supposes that the Son of God is to be glorified by the manifestation of creative power in raising Lazarus from the dead. But I believe a suggestion put forward by the Rev. Warburton Lewis for the understanding of this passage is to be preferred. In the sequel we read that 'from that day on the chief priests and the Pharisees took counsel how to put Him to death'. In John's gospel, the raising of Lazarus is the proximate cause of Christ's death, and so this illness was the means of the Son of God being glorified.

In chapter 13, the association of ideas is again unmistakable. When Judas rises from the supper table and passes out into the night to betray his Master, Jesus says, 'Now is the Son of Man glorified and in Him God is glorified.' Nothing can now hinder the train of events which the action of Judas will set in motion. God will be glorified by the Son's perfect obedience to His Father's will. 'The cup which My Father hath given me, shall I not drink it?' And the Son of Man is glorified, at the moment when He can say, 'It is finished'.

Schmiedel in his article on the Gospels in the *Encyclopaedia Biblica* made an interesting comment on verse 30 in John 19, which speaks of the actual death of Christ. The verse runs: 'When Jesus had received the wine, He said "It is finished"; and He bowed His head and gave up His spirit.' Schmiedel pointed out that the Greek phrase, translated here 'He bowed His head', is paralleled only in the saying, 'The Son of Man hath not where to *rest His head*'. Perhaps we should adopt this rendering in John. 'There is pathos and power in the thought that the one place on earth where the Son of Man "rested His head" was the Cross, and the one moment was when He had accomplished the Father's will.'

Christ's death then is Christ's glory. The Cross, once the symbol of shame and weakness has become the standard of power and glory. 'In the Cross of Christ, I glory, Towering o'er the wrecks of time. All the light of sacred story, Gathers round its head sublime.' And the Cross is the foundation of Christ's enduring empire in the hearts of men. The comment of General Booth on the passage in Mark, describing the mockery of the bystanders on Calvary—'save yourself and come down from the cross!'—is relevant here.

'They would have believed in Him if He had come down; we believe in Him, because He stayed up.'

What then is the connection between Jesus being glorified and the gift of the Spirit? The evangelist suggests that only after Jesus had been glorified could the disciples appreciate the meaning of the teaching they had received and of the incidents they had witnessed. He says this expressly of the entry into Jerusalem, recorded in chapter 12. 'His disciples did not understand this at first; but when Jesus was glorified, they remembered . . .' More generally, we can see that the Spirit of God which is the Spirit of love could not move freely in the hearts of men until love had been manifested in its fullness on the Cross. For the gospel is not accurately summarised in the words 'God is love', but rather in the phrase 'God so loved that He gave'. As Mr. Basil Willey says in his new book *Christianity, Past and Present*, 'Christianity admittedly was not founded only on the discovery that God is love; it began in the faith that God had shown His love once for all in a unique historical fact.' So John concludes in his epistle, 'Beloved,—if God so loved us, we also ought to love one another'.

XI

THE MINISTRY OF RECONCILIATION

Text for study: 2 *Corinthians* $5^{18\text{-}21}$

OUR key passage is in St. Paul's second letter to the Corinthians. It runs thus: 'God in Christ was reconciling the world to Himself, not counting their trespasses against them and entrusting to us the message of reconciliation. On Christ's behalf then we are ambassadors as though God were making His appeal through us. We beseech you, on behalf of Christ, be ye reconciled to God. Him who knew no sin, God made to be sin for our sakes, that we in Him may become the righteousness of God.'

It is important to note that the initiative here is God's initiative. Christ did not die to persuade God to be reconciled to us men. He died to persuade us men to be reconciled to God. This is, of course, a paradox. God might well order or summon men to repent, as Paul himself suggested when he spoke on Mars' Hill. But in Christ, God begs and beseeches us to be reconciled to Himself. You would expect sinners to plead with God to be reconciled to them, but the ambassadors for Christ plead with sinners to be reconciled to God. The significance of this appeal is well brought out in a few sentences from a sermon by John Oman in the volume recently published, entitled *A Dialogue with God*. 'This is a revelation of God Himself. He beseeches, He will not, cannot compel. This is what the revelation of God in Christ says, God will do everything for man, suffer everything for him, give everything for him, but He will not override his will. If He cannot have free service He cares for no other. Just because He would do so much for man to draw him, it is clear that He could not compel him. Peace must be of the heart and will or it is nothing. The reason why the Cross of Christ means so much is just that God beseeches us in it by every sacrifice love can offer, and tells us that He can only beseech, He cannot compel.' This comment of John Oman's reminds us that God's thoughts are not as our thoughts—When *we* are offended, we often say we are willing to forgive the offender, if he first shows a proper contrition and takes the first step towards reconciliation. We cannot be expected to make a move ourselves. The Cross means not only that God has taken the first step but that He has done all that is needed or possible from His side to reconcile us to Himself. This is made clear in the phrases in Romans, chapter 5. 'While we were still weak and helpless, at the right time Christ died for the ungodly . . .' 'God commends His love toward us in that while we were still sinners, Christ died for us.' 'While we were still sinners'—that is, before we had repented and confessed our sins. 'While we were enemies we have been reconciled to God by the death of His Son.' Weak, godless, sinners, enemies—it is an ascending scale of alienation from God, but wherever men stand on this scale, Christ has died for them. God makes His offer of forgiveness, before we have repented, to persuade us to repent.

'Be ye reconciled to God.' The reconciliation will vary with our attitudes. If we are consumed with fears, Christ bids us fear not. If we are conscious of our guilt and unworthiness, Christ bids us come boldly to the throne of grace. But in many minds, the obstacle to reconciliation is that we have a grudge against God. We refuse to be reconciled to reality. We quarrel with God's ordering of our lives. There is, of course, such a thing as divine discontent. There are conditions we are meant to alter, and limitations we are entitled to challenge. But there is a much vaster element of discontent which is not divine, discontent which comes from thinking of ourselves more highly than we ought to think, discontent compounded of jealousy and envy of our neighbours, and resentment against God's apparent ill-treatment of us. Christ died to *disarm* such resentment, to *win over* such enemies. Again, there is the stubborn self-assertiveness, which refuses God's guidance. We want to be the captains of our souls, the masters of our fate. Christ died to convince us that in God's service is perfect freedom. Then finally there are those who wish to control not only their own lives, but other people's lives. *God* may beseech, but *they* will compel their fellows, for their own good, of course. We have the experts who are ready to plan our lives for us, and the Marxists who are so sure that they are right that they can't wait to persuade us. They would play providence over history and usurp the place of God. Christ died to save us from this kind of insolent self-confidence. Christ died to undermine this and all other forms of human pride. 'Hold we our heads never so high, they shall be bowed at the last.'

In the letter to the Ephesians, St. Paul speaks of the mystery of Christ, which he understands to be the discovery that the Gentiles are fellow-heirs, members of the same body and partakers of the promise in Christ Jesus through the gospel. Christ's death is to reconcile men to God. It is also to reconcile men to men. The Gentiles are fellow heirs with the Jews. For St. Paul this is bound up with the thought that Christ's death by ending the claim of the Law has broken down the middle wall of partition, the iron curtain, that separated Jews and Gentiles. Christ has made possible our peace with God. He has also made possible peace between races, nations and classes. He is our peace, and 'if we walk in the light as He is in the light, we have fellowship with one another and the blood of Jesus, God's son, cleanses us from every kind of sin'. Fellowship with our fellowmen must be rooted in reconciliation to God. The beloved community cannot be realised on any other basis.

XII

SOME PRACTICAL CONCLUSIONS

Texts for study: 1 *Corinthians* 6^{20}, 8^{3}, 1 *John* 4^{11}

'THE life that I now live in the flesh I live by faith in the Son of God who loved me and gave Himself for me.' Thus St. Paul announced his faith for living. No doubt this faith had become a real power in his life, because he had encountered the risen Christ on the Damascus road. Yet it was a faith he was prepared to commend to others, a faith that all might share. Others have lived by this faith with the same intensity of devotion. Listen to St. Francis Xavier.

> Thou, O my Jesus, Thou didst me
> Upon the Cross embrace;
> For me didst bear the nails and spear
> And manifold disgrace;
> And griefs and torments numberless
> And sweat of agony
> E'en death itself and all for one
> Who was thine enemy.
> Then why, O blessed Jesus Christ
> Should I not love Thee well?

This was the inspiration of this other great apostle to the Gentiles. Take a more recent instance of a discovery of the same faith for living. That remarkable woman Simone Weil in her book *Waiting on God* tells something of her spiritual autobiography. She suffered a great deal from ill-health, but often at the culminating point of a violent headache, she would recite George Herbert's poem 'Love'—the poem which begins 'Love bade me welcome: yet my soul drew back, Guiltie of dust and sinne'. She wrote 'I make myself say it over, concentrating all my attention upon it and clinging with all my soul to the tenderness it enshrines. . . . It was during one of these recitations that Christ Himself came down and took possession of me. . . . In this sudden possession of me by Christ, neither my senses nor my imagination had any part: I only felt in the midst of my suffering the presence of a love, like that which one can read in the smile of a beloved face.'

Those who know the poem will not be surprised that it should lead, in the case of Simone Weil, to a revelation of the Son of God, who loved her and gave Himself for her.

Such experiences may be rare indeed, but we may all share this faith. Whether we like it or not, whether we are aware of it or not, we have all been bought with a price. We are often unconscious or oblivious of our debt to Christ. Yet as my friend, Thomas Edmunds, says, 'A man cannot grow up within English culture without being in touch with that which is Christ.' If we were fully aware of the sources of what is best in our make-up, everyone of us would need to include in his or her autobiography a chapter headed, 'What I owe to Christ'. 'Did we see how needful Christ is to us, we should esteem and love Him more.'

The true appreciation of human worth is bound up with our faith in the Son of God who loved us and gave Himself for us. We learn to reverence ourselves when we remember that we have been bought with a price. We learn to respect our fellowmen when we remember that they are brothers for whom Christ died. The Cross stands between us and a relapse into barbarism, that nasty, poor, brutish state of nature from which Leviathan was to rescue us. But the state is not the Saviour. Our only shield and protector is Christ crucified.

T. R. Glover liked to recall historic occasions when the appeal to this sense of human worth has been strikingly made. There is the example of the good bishop, Synesius, rebuking a new Roman governor of Cyrenaica about A.D. 410, who was oppressing the people. 'The governor was treating human beings as if they were cheap, but said Synesius "Man is a thing of price, for Christ died for him".' Again there is Kett the rebel-leader in Norfolk answering the court's emissary with the words, 'Call not these men villeins for whom Christ died.' Glover adds, 'The very phrase chimes through the Christian centuries and it has been a charter of the oppressed through the ages.'

This faith in the Son of God who loved us and gave Himself for us is the enduring faith of the social reformer. One who lives by this faith can never treat his fellowmen as things, as means to his ends. He will never be deceived by the logic of the totalitarian regimes whose rulers are prepared to sacrifice any number of other people's lives for the sake of their experiments. All tyranny and oppression are undermined, where the love of Christ is known and trusted. And this faith commits those who live by it to give the last measure of devotion in the service of their fellows for Christ's sake. 'Beloved,—if it was thus that God loved us, we ought also so to love one another.'

We cannot escape this challenge, though few of us can face it. 'Many go with the Lord to the breaking of the bread, but few to the drinking of the cup of His passion.' One of the most pathetic utterances in the gospels is the reply of the sons of Zebedee to their Master's question: 'Are ye able to drink of the cup that I shall drink?' In their innocence they answered, 'We are able.' But most of us will echo a poem from Rabindranath Tagore's *Gitanjali*.

'When I try to bow to thee, my obeisance cannot reach down to the depth where thy feet rest among the poorest and lowliest and lost. . . .

'My heart can never find its way to where thou keepest company with the companionless among the poorest, the lowliest and the lost.'

Of ourselves we are incapable of the heroism which the sons of Zebedee so lightly assumed. We follow afar off and with faltering steps. But we may remember for our encouragement that the least little service for His sake, the cup of cold water in His name, is accepted by Him. His love for us, not our love for Him is the basis of our hope and confidence. And each of us may say:

> Lord, it is my chief complaint
> That my love is weak and faint:
> Yet I love Thee and adore,
> Oh, for grace to love Thee more.